In The Street

Kath Cox and Pat Hughes

Wayland

Notes for Parents and Teachers

This book provides a flexible teaching resource for Early Years history. Two levels of text are given – a simple version and a more advanced and extended level. The book can be used for:

◆ Early stage readers at Key Stage 1
◆ Older readers needing differentiated text
◆ Non-readers who can use the photographs
◆ Extending skills of reading non-fiction
◆ Adults reading aloud to provide a model for non-fiction reading

By comparing photographs from the past and the present, children are able to develop skills of observation, ask questions and discuss ideas. They should begin by identifying the familiar in the modern photographs before moving on to the photographs from the past. The aim is to encourage children to make 'now' and 'then' comparisons.

The use of old photographs not only provides an exciting primary resource for history but, used alongside the modern photographs, aids the discussion of the development of photography. Modern photographs in black and white are included to encourage children to look more closely at the photographs and avoid seeing the past as 'black and white'. All the historical photographs were taken beyond the living memory of children and most have been selected from the Edwardian period between 1900–1920. A comprehensive information section for teachers, parents and other adults on pages 29–31 gives details of each of the old photographs, where known, and suggests points to explore and questions to ask children.

Editors: Dereen Taylor and Joanna Bentley
Designer: Michael Leaman
Production Controller: Carol Stevens
Consultant: Suzanne Wenman

Front cover: The main photograph is of a street in Somerset in about 1910.
The inset photograph is of a high street in the 1990s.
Endpapers: Photographers at work at a wedding, 1907.
Title page: The London Fire Brigade, about 1900.

Picture Acknowledgements
The publishers would like to thank the following for allowing their pictures to be used in this book: Beamish, The North of England Open Air Museum 25; Angus Blackburn 8, 26; Mary Evans Picture Library 9; Sally and Richard Greenhill **cover inset**, 12; Hulton Deutsch Collection title page, 5, 7, 11, 13, 15; Impact Photos Ltd 20, 22, 24; Tizzie Knowles 6, 18; Billie Love Historical Collection 19; Royal Photographic Society contents page, endpapers, 17; Tony Stone Worldwide 10; Topham Picture Source **cover main**, 14, 21, 27, Warrington Museum and Art Gallery 23; Wayland Picture Library 16; Zefa Picture Library 4.

First published in 1996 by Wayland (Publishers) Limited
61 Western Road, Hove, East Sussex BN3 1JD, England

© Copyright 1996 Wayland (Publishers) Limited

The right of Kath Cox and Pat Hughes to be identified as the authors of this work has been asserted in accordance with the Copyright, Designs and Patents Act 1988.

British Library Cataloguing in Publication Data
Cox, Kath
In the Street. – (History from Photographs Series)
I. City and town life – History – Juvenile literature
2. Streets – History – Juvenile literature
1. Title II. Hughes, Pat, 1933-388.4'11'09

ISBN 0-7502-1543-7

Typeset in the UK by Michael Leaman Design Partnership
Printed and bound in Great Britain by B.P.C. Paulton Books Ltd

·Contents·

A Brownie box camera and case, 1900.

Some of the more difficult words appear in the text in **bold**.
These words are explained in the picture glossary on page 28.
The pictures will help you to understand the entries more easily.

Oxford Street is a busy street in London.

There are many buses and taxis on the road.

The surface of the street is made of tarmac.

Traffic lights, signs and **road markings** help to direct drivers.

People walk on wide **pavements**.

Oxford Street was busy 100 years ago.

Most **vehicles** at this time were pulled by horses.
There were no traffic lights and few road signs.
The road was made of **cobble stones** set close together.

This shop is in a special street where cars cannot go.

Some towns have shopping areas where the streets
are mainly for **pedestrians**.
Delivery vans or lorries are allowed in the street
at special times of the day.
Pedestrianized streets like this are safer for shoppers.

Streets were not as busy as today.

There was less traffic on the roads.
The car had only just been invented and vehicles moved more slowly.
Most people walked or cycled to work and to the shops.

Mrs Campbell owns this shop.

She sells sweets, groceries, newspapers and many other things.

Most of her customers live near the shop.

Many families prefer to drive to a supermarket to do their shopping.

There was a general store in most large streets.

This kind of shop sold many different things, but most other shops at this time were small and sold one type of **goods**.

Some towns have a market in the main street.

The **stalls** are put up early in the morning and taken down at night.
Traffic has to be directed along other roads.
In many places the market has been moved to a special site
away from the busy streets.

Most towns and villages had a street market.

The market was held in the main street every week.
People travelled into the town from the countryside on Market Day.
They did their shopping and met their friends.

This street trader sells ice-cream from a van.

Music plays to tell people that the ice-cream seller is in the street.
The driver stops the van to sell ice-cream.
Then he drives on to the next street.

Ice-cream was sold from hand carts in the street.

Many different kinds of food could be bought in the streets.
Traders shouted to let people know what they could buy.
Many children worked as street sellers.

Dave and Rob play music in the street.

This is called busking.

Buskers entertain people in the street and can be found in many towns.

People stop to listen and give them money.

There were different kinds of entertainers in the street.

Street organs were popular.
Music played when a handle on the organ was turned and the monkeys danced and collected money from the audience.
Street entertainers moved from one street to another.

Post boxes are found in many streets.

Most are made of iron and painted red. Some post boxes are a hundred years old. Post boxes, **litter** bins, signs and bus shelters are all things found in the street.

There were post boxes in the street 100 years ago.

The first post box was put up in 1852. It had six sides and was made of iron.

Michael delivers newspapers.

People pay the **newsagent** to have papers and magazines brought to their homes.
Sometimes newspapers are sold from stands in the street.

This man sold newspapers in the street.

Customers stopped him when they wanted to buy a paper.
Many different goods were brought to homes by delivery boys
riding bicycles with large baskets fixed to the front.

Mr. Morton is a street cleaner.

People and traffic make the streets dirty and untidy.
Special machines are used to pick up the rubbish.
Dirt and litter are sucked up from the road into a bag.

Street cleaners worked
with brushes and **shovels**.

Streets in towns were often dirty and muddy.
Women with long skirts had to be careful as they walked across the road.

There are road-works in this street.

The street is being re-surfaced.

Busy roads are damaged and worn out by traffic.

Potholes and cracks appear in the road surface.

Most of the repair work is done by machines.

Many new roads were built.

The invention of the petrol engine meant that more vehicles travelled on the roads.

More roads were needed to link the new houses being built.

Men did most of the work by hand.

These men are mending a street light.

Street lighting makes roads safer for pedestrians and traffic.
The lights are electric and switch on and off automatically.
Street lights have to be checked and repaired regularly.

The streets in many towns were lit by gas lamps.

Lamplighters lit the gas in the street lamps when it got dark.
In the morning they turned off the gas and the light went out.
Some of the bigger houses had gas lighting too.

· Index ·

(Items that appear in text)